D1266003

OCEAN HUNTERS

UNDER THE SEA

Lynn M. Stone

Rourke Publishing LLC
Vero Beach, Florida 32964

www.rourkepublishing.com

PHOTO CREDITS:
All photographs ©Marty Snyderman except pgs 7, 13, 21 ©Lynn M. Stone

EDITORIAL SERVICES:
Pamela Schroeder

Library of Congress Cataloging-in-Publication Data

Stone, Lynn M.
    Ocean Hunters / Lynn M. Stone.
        p. cm. — (Under the sea)
    Includes bibliographical references (p.).
    ISBN 1-58952-111-0
    1. Predatory marine animals—Juvenile literature. [1. Predatory animals. 2. Marine animals.] I. Title.

QL122.2 .S793 2001
591.77—dc21   2001019425

Printed in the USA

TABLE OF CONTENTS

OCEAN HUNTERS

Many animals of the sea kill other animals for food. These hunting animals are ocean **predators**. The animals they hunt are their **prey**.

One of the ocean's biggest and best-known predators is the great white shark. Another is the orca, or killer whale.

Marine predators must kill prey to live. Without prey, they would die.

The great white shark is one of the ocean's largest and most powerful predators.

PREY

Each kind of predator usually eats more than one kind of prey. For example, young great white sharks eat mostly rays and fish. Older great whites eat larger fish. They also eat marine **mammals**. Seals and sea lions are two of the marine mammals that great white sharks eat.

Lemon sharks feed on fish. Scalloped hammerhead sharks feed on squid and small fish. Leopard seals sometimes eat penguins.

Killer whales hunt for salmon along the coast of British Columbia.

Some of the largest marine animals feed on very small animals. The whale shark is the largest fish on Earth. It grows to 40 feet (12 meters) in length. The whale shark lives on **plankton**. Plankton is a floating "stew" of tiny marine animals and plants.

Shrimp-sized krill are a favorite prey of big animals such as seals, penguins, and whales. The blue whale is the largest animal ever. Almost 9,000 pounds (4,000 kilograms) of krill have been found in the stomach of one blue whale!

A huge whale shark feeds on tiny plankton.

HOW PREDATORS HUNT

Plankton and krill hunters can just swim into great clouds of their prey and chomp away. But for the true predators, hunting is a skill.

Many big predators use speed and their powerful, toothy jaws to catch prey. These big marine predators usually have smooth, slender bodies that move quickly through the sea.

A California sea lion swims into a school of silvery baitfish.

11

A sunflower star attacks smaller brittle stars.

Numbers of certain North Pacific fish have dropped and so have numbers of the Steller's sea lions that prey upon them.

Not all marine predators chase their prey. The wobbegong shark of the Indian Ocean hunts from **camouflage**. The wobbegong's colors match the ocean bottom where it lives. Prey fish don't see the hidden wobbegong. When prey swims close, the wobbegong grabs it.

A spotted wobbegong hunts by hiding on the ocean floor.

The sawshark may have one of the world's most unusual hunting styles. Scientists think the sawshark catches small fish on the saw-like "teeth" of its long snout.

Several smaller marine predators hunt with their **tentacles**. Tentacles stretch from animal-like fingers, snake-like arms, or long threads. Many jellyfish and sea **anemones** have tentacles that sting. When a small fish brushes against a tentacle, the stings kill or injure it.

The unusual snout of a sawshark is probably used to slash into schools of fish.

The most famous tentacles in the sea belong to the octopus. The octopus may hunt from hiding or make a quick dash through the water. Octopus tentacles do not sting. But the octopus does have **venom** in its bite. Venom is a type of poison. Sea snakes are other marine animals that have venom.

An octopus feeds on a soft snail inside its shell.

FINDING PREY

A predator can kill—and eat—only if it can find prey. Predators use their eyes when they can. But sunlight doesn't reach deep into water. In deep water, eyes are of little use.

Dolphins use **echolocation** instead of their eyes. A dolphin makes clicking sounds. When the sound reaches an object, it echoes back to the dolphin. The echo tells the dolphin where the objects are and in what direction they're going. It's like having a built-in fish finder!

Sharks don't have echolocation, but they have a great sense of smell.

Dolphin chatter undersea helps these predators and their relatives find fish prey.

THE LARGEST MARINE PREDATORS

The largest marine predators are whales. The biggest marine fish predators are sharks and ocean sunfish.

The largest seal is the southern elephant seal. It can weigh up to 8,100 pounds (3,700 kg) on its diet of fish and squid.

The leatherback is the largest marine turtle. It is a jellyfish hunter. The leatherback can weigh more than 2,000 pounds (900 kg).

The emperor penguin is the largest marine bird predator. The emperor can weigh more than 90 pounds (40 kg).

GLOSSARY

anemone (an EM on ee) — a kind of soft, simple, marine animal with tentacles

camouflage (KAM eh flahj) — the ability of an animal to blend into its surroundings

echolocation (ek oh loh KAY shen) — a way of locating objects by sending out sounds and receiving their echoes

mammal (MAM el) — an animal in the group of air-breathing, warm-blooded, milk-producing animals with hair or fur

marine (meh REEN) — of the sea

plankton (PLANGK ten) — the usually tiny, floating plants and animals of the seas

predator (PRED eh tor) — an animal that kills other animals for food

prey (PRAY) — an animal that is hunted by another animal for food

tentacles (TEN te kelz) — a group of long, flexible body parts that usually grow around an animal's mouth and are used for touching, grasping, or stinging

venom (VEN em) — the poison made by some animals

INDEX

Further Reading

Cerullo, Mary. *The Truth about Great White Sharks*. Chronicle Books, 2000

Marquitty, Miranda. *Shark*. Dorling Kindersley, 2000

Mitchell, Carolyn B. *Who's For Dinner?* Discovery Communications, 1998

Seward, H. *Frightening Fish* Rourke Publishing, 1998

Websites To Visit

- www.ds.dial.pipex.com/sharktrust/why.shtml
- www.top20biology.com

About The Author

Lynn Stone is the author of over 400 children's books. He is a talented natural history photographer as well. Lynn, a former teacher, travels worldwide to photograph wildlife in their natural habitat.

10|02